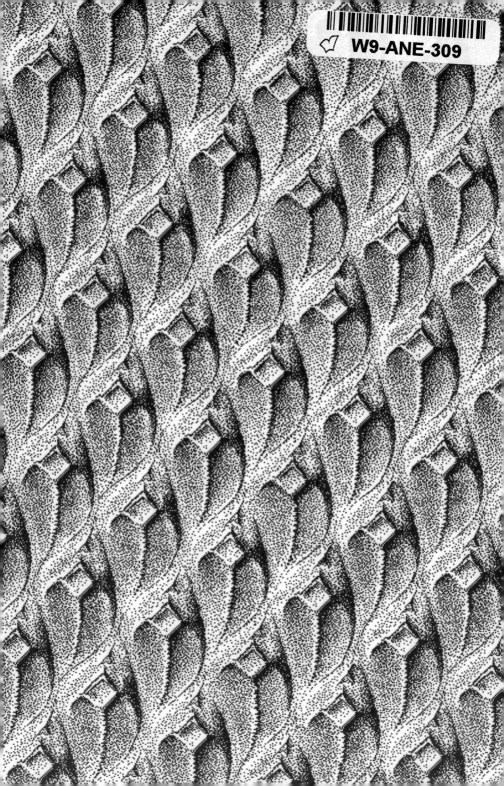

THE NATURAL HISTORY
Christopher Dewdney

MISFIT

Published by ECW PRESS
2120 Queen Street East, Suite 200, Toronto, Ontario, Canada M4E IE2

NATIONAL LIBRARY OF CANADA CATALOGUING IN PUBLICATION DATA

Dewdney, Christopher, 1951–
The natural history : poems

ISBN 1-55022-513-8

I. Nature–Poetry. I. Title.

PS8557.E846N37 2002   C811'.54   C2001-904070-9
PR9199.3.D48N37 2002

Editor: Michael Holmes, a misFit book
Cover and Text design: Darren Holmes
Production: Mary Bowness
Printing: Marc Veilleux Imprimeur INC.
Author photo: Derek Shapton
Front cover: Darren Holmes

This book is set in Garamond

2nd Edition

The publication of *The Natural History* has been generously supported by the Canada Council, the Ontario Arts Council, and the Government of Canada through the Book Industry Development Program. Canadä

Spring Trances, *The Cenozoic Asylum* and *Concordat Proviso Ascendant* were first published by The Figures in Berkeley, California and Great Barrington, Massachusetts. *Spring Trances*, *The Cenozoic Asylum* and *Concordat Proviso Ascendant* were subsequently republished by McClelland and Stewart, Toronto. *Permugenesis* was published by Nightwood Editions. *TimeWind* was first published by McClelland and Stewart. Excerpts from *The Natural History* have appeared in *Grand Street*, *Matrix*, *Poetry Canada Review*, *The Long Poem Anthology* and elsewhere.

DISTRIBUTION

CANADA: Jaguar Book Group, 100 Armstrong Avenue, Georgetown, ON   L7G 5S4

PRINTED AND BOUND IN CANADA

ECW PRESS
ecwpress.com

Contents

ACKNOWLEDGEMENTS

Initial thanks go to Geoffrey Young, who published the first three books of *The Natural History* with The Figures press in Berkeley, California and in Great Barrington, Massachusetts. Thanks also to Dennis Lee, who was the editor for the first two books of *The Natural History* at McClelland and Stewart, and to Ellen Seligman, who subsequently oversaw the production of three books of *The Natural History* at McClelland and Stewart. I must also acknowledge David Lee and Maureen Cochrane at Nightwood Editions who published *Permugenesis*. Much thanks is due to the editors who have worked with me on this project, most recently Stan Dragland and Barbara Gowdy. I am also indebted to Michael Holmes at ECW who originally proposed this collection and who contributed both editorial and practical support. I thank the Canada Council, the Ontario Arts Council and the Toronto Arts Council for their invaluable assistance during the writing of this book.

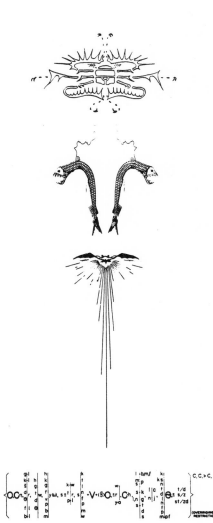

PART I
Spring Trances
(1974–1975)

August's amniotic haze is our dream
aether, our lens of distance. Every tree
an island with vicious night flowering
in the inky strata of sexual vision. The
portentous rumbling of far storms.
Limestone corridors inside stone libraries
dream the hot, grey rainless days of August.
The Niagara forest opens before us
in an opulent Fragonard brain-coral,
spotted with sun. Autumn the colour of
light these leaves absorbed in the summer
spectrum each had witnessed.

Dolomite temple walls rise from
a prehistoric lily pond, trickling water
leaving limestreaks out of pale green,
oxidized copper tubes. Luna moths
cluster in a corner of the pond, fading
into the dream's edge.

Here at the planetary surface our voices
dissolve, some hand or shadow moving
through the words.

Someone standing behind us.

There are two worlds – one diurnal
and that other world, where lunar
mottled eels stir like dreams in shallow
forest water. Allowing both to continue,
we painstakingly remove and replace their
parts with corresponding and interlocking
absences. The glass machinery equally full
of allusion to our summer carnality,
an infinite part of the pattern
that regenerates itself with its own
repetitive logic.

Triassic afternoons in early October.

Each huge spring bud is a pregnant
chrysalis unfolding into bat-wings. Every
nuance plotted in radar-tunnels.
The secrecy of your voice behind me
in a crowd, alarms like remoras, vacuous
and cold lurking in the eddies
of your passing.

The air is water.

The skin, neither moist nor dry,
is a porous membrane of cells dividing
the summer landscape into pink and blue.
Spring aches in the heart and stomach,
the surfacing of women in moist soil
and moonlight.

There is a darkness outside of those
confined to light. We are strangers
here in the fiction of our own hearts

The source a distant thunder in August.
Cumulonimbus incus. Fetal storm clouds
at dusk, pink intrusions of stone within sky.
Fantastic coral reefs forming on the horizon.

Rumblings from the earth.

Land breaking like rotten spring ice
into light.

She stares at a glacial lake. Her vision
grows flowers on plants. The musicians,
their divine arguments.

A cephalopod washes up on a grey Silurian
beach. There are no land plants and little
oxygen in the atmosphere. On the sandy
riverbanks pebbles of edible beige limestone
are frosted with fossil crinoids. The sand
granular orange from ant excavations
sliding, drying in the sun.

Purple and lime the Brazilian night,
as jewelled insects bead the lights.

The glistening highlight continuous
through all living creatures. August
refracted in the etched crystal of erosion.
Limestone caverns hold captive the slow
organic branchings of the glass machinery.
A molten intrusion of love solidifies
into a stone tree. Its leaves blow
in some hollow interglacial autumn
to the Scarborough bluffs.

The light in these afternoons is the reverse
of morning. Who can truly tell dawn
from dusk?

There is a path for you here if you see it.

Form of the graceful white elms
that flowered everything beneath
and translated it perfectly. An automobile
glides through night elm corridors
– its green instrument panel
phosphorescent beneath the manifold
of darkness. The valley filled with slow
motion wind and haze and golden
– the sun in clear warm water. Asphalt
oozes out of the ground.

The forest is filled with eyes, clear

unblinking surprises – intelligence
formulates its own disguises.

A Tantric delight and warm the micro-
climatic inclusion of our electric bodies,
currency the wind lends to oceans
of leaves. Our white palms pressed
together. There is a home in Northern
Ontario. Summer wasteland, June,
limestone village park blending
into country and the moon arena.
At Bayfield the White Sands testing blue
sky with the clarity of aerospace suspends
a remote, far-flung jet. No contrail,
no clouds, no earth. One soon loses
the sensation of falling. The wisdom
of her lineaments curl and vanish
into the landscape. Tall red oaks, bilateral
clouds of English coal and limestone
smoke in 1908. Corridors of gigantic
industrial elms, Egyptian in the motionless
stadium heat of August. Moss and rain
on limestone with milk snakes and milk
sliding couples.

It all happens quite rapidly.

The land is honeycombed with entrances
to caverns.

A drama of bark. A large room

in an ancient museum with walls papered
in a stage rendition of a forest. The forest
is naked. Pompeii. The pad of feet
on packed soil, her flesh on humus
and nipples erect with bits of leaf stuck
to them. Squatting patiently all night
after a rain as a large toadstool rises up
into her vagina. Orange toadstool
of immense budding inside her.
Her molluscan pool.

Small cumulus clouds momentarily
darken white rooms as they pass above
the mansions of Forest Hill. Salamanders'
viscous throats pulsating beneath rocks
as the intimate order of life continues
in silence and without witness. Space
solidifies into limestone each time
the entire perceptual memory of a life
becomes trapped in the sediments. The dim
pop of a weather Zonde clicks
in the high, thin air of the ionosphere.

Peace at this point. The dry, whispering
celluloid grass. At night lights the insects
gather in their teak and obsidian regalia
of summer foliage – this meaning
not camouflage but magnification.

Pit vipers.

Two pilots sweat with the tension
and precision of their task. Infra-red
snakes sway at night in the desert,
the air intoxicates our eyes, never quite open
enough for the detail.

And touching you, my fingers became water,
dispersing porous into the foliage
of your nervous system.

Each sound rings the silence formed
as a sphere around it. The heat wave
submerges the river's vegetation in a mute
bell of psilocybic thickness. Events occur
linearly, so densely they seem simultaneous.
Our senses trail in Lemur-fingers
and areolisma. The earth extends thin
electric tendrils up through the soles
of our feet to clutch our stomachs nervously.
Our eyes ascribe some golden instruction
dictated by the late afternoon sun.
The evidence constantly reassembles itself
and is testimony and judgment,
as the punishment for the fall from awareness
is the fall itself. Directions are indicated
by detail, open at either end. The water
glistens digitally in the computer sunlight.
Rain descends over erect cocks and nipples.

The Springbank soil clings to her thighs.

The story-book blue night unfolds
in a dark vacuous dream around the trees
in the city park. Sperm on swollen lips
in the full noon sun. Cocks semi-
transparent in foliage of vein
and translucent head the cool vagina under
camera tree. The night siphons mirror
and chrome into itself from the machines
that skim the day-warm asphalt.
Electochemicals transmitted through moist
air with endless erotic throttles. Serotonin
drips from wet leaves while bats flutter
through the abiogenetic night sky.

The limestone houses of Kingston
are small chapels preserving the fertility
of the White Elm. Night insects cross
the 401 – mists near escarpment farms.
Black River limestone. Persian Milky Way
and small maples with huge leaves.
Mulberry tunnels and open pavilions.
Spring trances in the control emerald night.

Silent lightning strikes close in a rainless
storm. Electric magneto purples
and the leaves, green stroboscopic,
transform into star clusters. Frozen silver
statue of a jaguar glints in the retina
of a Mayan astronomer. The irresistible

current of the approaching storm.
Herculaneum frozen. Arkona frozen.
Molecules preserved in stone the single
crystal of genetic light. The choice must
not be conceived, else it is made.

Furniture vacant of figures.

Space constricted by the passage of time.

Dundas observatory submerged in deepest
limousine navy. Tiers of orange-lit
apartments and older women not yet
opaque in the vacancy of pubescent dreams.
A loose-jointed reptilian homing-device
approaches like a blind-spot through
the articulation and splendour of the tree-
ferns. The forest rejoices at night
in the synergy of its intentions. In the next
tent, dimly, I can hear the sounds
of weeping babies preparing to be born.

Some hand or shadow moving through
the words. Fossils brought into a kind
of relief. Interface of limestone and spring
sky, the matrix evaporating.

Windy summer noon – no humans,
the cold vacant sun – Chinese leaves
flutter in alien wholeness on bending
and illumined boughs.

The pond is optical jelly, a retinal forest
cut by the long cool rays
of the afternoon sun. It is hollow
– look at it and you exist both within
and without in an eternally recurring
sequence. Aspic water dyed by cedar
tannin, empty of microscopic life. At night
red and feebly glowing molecular clusters
dance in slow gyrations near the pond's
surface, randomly illuminating the lower
boughs of cedar trees. By day the pond
increases ten fathoms in depth, a ceaseless
dark at the bottom where decaying cedar
leaves and twigs form indecipherable
hieroglyphs in the cat-fish murk.

The council of dreams takes place
in a nocturnal chamber where a thousand
perfect faces converge into a white, cranial
haze. Twilight. The rude, honest gaze
of the observer falls upon a woman near
the edge of the forest. How easily
the invisible camera shifts into his eyes.
Deep in the shadows and soft sourceless
light of dream he remembers a cavern,
a fictional labyrinth of vision.

Local scarab beetles develop elaborate

horns and attachments.

There are places where the children leave
the larvae alone.

When I see her flesh budding I am
eviscerated with cool, hollow hands.
She is Hungry Hollow, a memory succubus
with her twelve-year-old grace. She
supervises wet dreams in Arkona.
She is fair, she is dark with leg tendons
that pull rock nerves under her soles
up demerara thighs and flash white
into the evening astonished.

In the night sky she composes its entirety
of interlocking replicas of herself.

The stars are mistakes yet to be opaqued
in the negative of creation.

In the dream city there is an aquarium
river. The stained glass windows
of boulevard homes glittering with vague
garden lusts. A hot moist climate
that engenders palmettos and umbrella
magnolias. Streets winding through
a labyrinth of parks, stone bridges, streams

and limestone outcroppings.
Earthquakes as frequent as the ominous
roar of flash floods.

We are just a step away from ourselves.
Wings of northern alloy clash high
in the vaulted and metallic night. Don't
turn around if the dark negative figure
following you up the stairs isn't yourself.
The bicycle is an exoskeleton, striding
magnification, snake chains and turgid
rubber on asphalt. Fossil fuel sunsets
through smoked glass.

Stars drip out of the cutaneous, erectile
velvet blue bandshell night — a full moon
with lavender areola. Bats investigate
houses like skin-divers nervously exploring
corals. Cecropia moths flutter on stiff
tissue wings — flitting shadows. The night
air arranges itself in thermal conglomerates
of cool and warm. Stone outcrops replay
the solar dictation.

Wet foliage.

Airport dawn. Vacant observation decks
reflect the radar-dishes, revolving
in the morning mist. Aerials glint
in the first light — orange translucent
against Persian blue.

There is nothing arbitrary
in the predestined universe of the past.
Emerald crystal caves in hot black tar.
Cloudy airport haze and warm afternoons.
A full moon passing behind fast night
clouds. Hot wind and moth tunnels traced
by pheromones. We are interminably
drawn to convergences over which forces
other than human preside.

I am walking south on Avenue Road.
Everything is working by remote control.

Snow clouds over the advance greens
of April, snow anticipated
in the shadows that sculpt the weathered
limestone blocks of universities and great
halls on the Niagara escarpment. Mansions
that later in May are obscured
by vegetation and haze, their night lights
visible from miles away among vine flats
extending from the foot of the cliff.
A sparse necklace of amber delineating
the crest of the escarpment. Annapolis
Royal an Atlantic echo. Statuary
and marble-tiled rose grottos lit by fireflies.
The air warm, yet quickened with altitude.
Airplane lights glowing red and green slide

into distant low fountains of artificial dawn.

Absolute July sun on white dolomite cliffs,
foliage boiling over the edge. Large homes
on outlying mesas – a praying mantis
at the cocktail party. In the early morning
light iridescent flower beetles lie drugged
at the foot of garden lamps. St. Mary's
quarry at night and the unearthly fish
that surface there. A woman crying inside
the moraine. Niagara Falls rumbling
just over the horizon, the electric lights
dimming and brightening in accordance
with its faint roar. Air thick with the smell
of peaches and grapes. Vacuum-tube larvae
coiling within the soil. Slender women
adorned with reticular pythons. In relaxing
liquid sensate knots the snakes uncoil.
Their scales susurrate in whispering loops –
beaded skin over limbo thighs. Below,
the dreamers walk through endless peach-
blossom orchards and erotic earth tremors.
The mansion parties go on all night.

Highway 403 – lush escarpment-plain
foliage, sassafras, pawpaw and tulip trees.
Patchy sunlight through thick mist
to the escarpment streaming
with vegetation and cumulonimbus
mounting behind. Cathedrals
and botanical gardens in intricate

profusion. The Dundas valley. Ferns
obscuring the lower windows of old country
homes. Far electrical factories
and medical-instruction buildings. Here
distance is not perspective, it is merely
out of reach. We portray ourselves perfectly,
a single divine skill.

The puffy silent flight of a car leaving
the escarpment highway at night. Small
boys amazed by dozens of meteors
and comets. April's stiletto rush is quickly
finished. The cold grey clouds do not bring
snow but move on.

Cisterns full of dark brown rainwater.
Limestone endless in detail.

Night trains and the transparent, barely
tangible young face drifting frictionless
just beyond our reflection in the coach
windows. And behind this weightless face
the corporeal body, streaming like a comet,
faint tapering blue remora on the side
of a segmented shark. Looking beyond
to the orange glow of farmhouse windows
– aquarium stories in the summer night.

P etrolia bathed in a neo-carboniferous
glow. Tar sands abound, pits with live
trapped smilodons snarling and surprisingly
lean. Limestone so soft that farmers feel
only a slight resistance as their ploughs
slice boulders in half. Fossils dragged
through rock like crumbs through butter.

Small prairies scattered across the
peninsula. Prickly pear cacti on Pelee Point
– egrets stilting through low glades –
crescent dunes in the early evening.
The sand is skin. Dozing raccoons sway
in gusts of wind high atop the beech trees
running over the escarpment's edge.

At noon the exposed limestone of the Paris
valley becomes a parabolic reflector
of atmospheric space focused inside
the stranger's brain. Jewelled sundews
on the floating bog. Pitcher plants
and tamarack with sphagnum moss
and an underground lake. Nighthawks
vigilant through the awesome stirring folds
of night. Flashing white bars on their
wings, their flights trace our most habitual
routes. Our dark luminous scents. Insect
metamorphosis proceeds. Leaves turn
into sparrows that fly away at the sound
of an approaching train. Its light shines
dimly around the curve of this hill.

I am told by a small old man to lie down
on the tracks and be crushed so my dreams
can begin.

Tropical storm cells follow the valley.
At its lip houses are exploded by lightning.
When our foreheads glide through each
other's symmetry, as far apart and identical
as colliding galaxies, the room breaks
into flashing white shards of interstellar
nothingness. This is no ordinary storm.
It is the dark and solipsistic cranial haze
around the spruce tops in the August
Quebec 1958 Niagara train-poster
moonlight. We are alone. Totally lonely,
totally lovely, totally omniscient. The sweet
desert of soul spreads its dark wings against
the stillness and poise of an August night.

Our seasons do not contaminate
the constellations.

The sun low and summer softly stabbing
you, as if you weren't quite sure when her
fingernails had pierced your skin. Forest
swamps cellophane green with duckweed
floors. Pawpaws rotting into the September
soil. The continuum in summer is a mature
expectation holding forth its mortality.
Great blue skinks – the waves of Erie
on white sand – thick subtropical forest

here at the dream's margin. Montreal
submerged just beyond Pelee Point. Canals
and abandoned fields of cantaloupe
and egrets. I am a certain woman,
she approaches me candidly at the edge
of clearing. Barely pubescent my breasts
are undeveloped and my penis seeks some
feline vagina. The lynx-padded forest floor
bathed in monsoon stained-glass northern
mineshaft star cathedral. Two birds fight
in mid-air, a suspended vortex of wing
and feather.

The mirror evaporates and the human
trapped in the other room crouches
and begins to approach your opening.
Eyes wide with fear.

There is a small lake in the Caledon hills
eternally immured in the vacuity
of a dry, sunny summer afternoon.
Its waves arranged in regular enameled sets
to match the China blue sky. Human eyes
do not graze here. Sunlight sparkling from
electronic water witnessed only by the dry
summer grass, celluloid blonde
and rippling. Nearby are deep carpeted
forests, mediaeval corridors opening

into a musk night inhabited by legendary
creatures.

We enter through a narrow underwater
tunnel. The flooded atrium is a pale blue-
green, its walls descend smoothly into body
temperature water. We hold hands
and explore the marine frescoes, the water
is clear as air.

PART 2
The Cenozoic Asylum
(1975–1981)

Wooden alveoli erect and fragile
in the rarefied air of October, leaves
frosted-glass, rock chapel orange and red.
The sky no longer enclosing us. The sound
of a distant airplane blossoming into clarity
and not enclosed. Eels pulled from
the canal. Even the planets are motile,
hoary with diamonds above the chiming
sunset. She swims alone and naked
in a clear October lake. A white building
stands free and O the spirits look dimly
out from there.

A light Modigliani orange as June evenings
are a pastel rainbow of dreams and mercury
vapour lamps, like giant mantids, just
coming on over the shopping plaza.
The violet and pink light setting tanned
skin aglow. Each muscle a new surrender.
The quiet village streets technologized
by our telephoto insignia, lush nightfall
still after a summer shower. The expectant
interglacial period gardens, their scale-speed
hierarchies squandered by darkness. Stars
arbitrate the carnivorous writhing
of cycads.

The pond magnifies its own refractive
distortion. Spring-fed, the precise internal
branches of underwater plants weave over
the pale, turquoise clay. Milky-green glass,

night conscious of itself, is secreted in large
fragments at the base of the cedars
surrounding the pond.

The elevator at Niagara Falls opens
to gardens on both levels. Floral dais.
The red image of the setting sun, opalized
through cirrus haze, reflected from car
windows. Insects, charmed particles
of dusk, orbit the sodium vapour lamps
above the expressway. The streetlights
menace the metal scuttling beneath
them like polished electric tear-drops.

Summer glen of green grass and tall cedar
and spruce. The spider's web beaded
with morning dew, an abacus
in the gravitational field of the moon.

The envelope of consciousness surrounded
by an aureole of dissolving nucleotides.
Glade solstice of the internal summer,
a tender explosion in the last enclave,
annihilate. Her nipples stiffen, flakes
of come peel off like cellophane. Her
delicate white legs unfoalding.

Each figment profound the music
is blown glass and cruelty turning
on some spit. Fired by the vast machinery
of the stars and their mysterious burning.
Each house encloses a novel dusk, turning
off all the lights. Windows open on both
sides to giant trees, still as dew
in the summer night. Water nymphs
enclose themselves in warm limestone
streams. Fireflies pinpoint cool luminous
ideas in the neural foliage of dreams.

Genital clusters. Leaf grotto.

A translucent Saturn, large as the moon,
ascends behind the vacant observatory.
In starlit fields unearthly children rehearse
an absent embrace.

The underwater archetype of your eternal
existence in sunlit brook chambers. Bend
sinister freed the broken consort.
And we built a temple in the warm night
air. The enormous hollyhock flower looms
paraboloid in the visual scan of the hover
fly. With cells shining gold rings and thin
amulets around the corporeal swarm.
The occasional giant thrusts through
the canopy, branches bending
in the rainless wind of a nocturnal heat
storm. The body is assembled around

the perceptions. Tiny iridescent bees.
The wind soft thunder in our ears. Reagent
command the word transcribed. Tactile
revelation of the optical sector. The anvil
tops of cumulonimbus graze
the stratosphere, moonlight high over
the storm witnessed by a small passenger
airliner lost in the thirties. Sucrose
in the infinite capillary network of the horse
chestnut, its sub-canopies dangling in ever-
rising cascades of green. Leafy strata under
which a forest sylph wends, so delicate she
could have been a rumour written in smoke.

Rivers of cool air flow in slow-motion
cascades down the ravines. The heavy air
slides beneath trees as bats inverting flicker
darkly through desire. Fascination drove
them into the shade. Aero-delta over
the river a shock-wave of mist.

One pure burning heart.

The body is a slow fire, an infra-red jungle
of thermal contours. The sun spiking
triangular fossil-jawed, the grain is blonde
and shimmering. The evening sun on a lone
crab-apple tree halfway up the side
of a bleached grassy hill, the blue windy sky.

In August there is a second spring,
bracken fiddleheads emerge in the north,
magnolias flower along the edge
of limestone chasms. Blossoming wasp
nests suspended like ash vortices bend their
boughs. Carnivals spawn as August hardens
into the fecund empire of September.
Leaves yellow and drop singly as in a rain
forest drought. Heat showers drive
the wasps from rotting peaches. Noctuids,
mantises, cicadas and dragonflies proliferate
as the insect population reaches its climax.
Small predatory night breezes rustle
through the undergrowth while striped
snails slumber beneath the leaves. Sweating
oak bannisters.

September is August enthroned. September
is August parentheticized.

Wired the first angelic rays spiking
horizontal above our heads. Pealing off
the line of evening in fluted stars. Tide
rising eventide to White Sands.

In a dream there is a basement.

Auto-erotic signals shimmer through buds
emerging red into green. Panther arrests
the pawpaw triumphant, July haze down
the lane, hanging gardens and old wood

in the garage. Giant scarab larvae, white
and translucent blue-stuffed saran jewels
in the hollow oak's loam. Coprolitic
chrysalis cases, grub-loam geodes
and the sculpted obsidian deities inside.
Pelidnota and Osmoderma. Brasilia,
harlequin nocturne. Giant flickering
scarabs orbit the night lights of a factory
in Manaus. All the machinery stands
poised and glistening. The nighthawks
return, a contracting pupil of magic
around the light-field of the city.
They are surveillance.

Burning the river dry the nights of forest
celebrations and softly glowing veins
of opal fluorescing in the clairvoyant
depths of limestone gorges.

The rain of sensorium is erosion
is the absolute event horizon exposing
memory. High relief from the rock matrix.
Form withstanding erosion. Fovea
Centralis now moving through the words.
Our actions tiny eddies and whirlpools
on the surface of a mirror-still planetary
ocean. Ripples indicate the stirrings
of Chinese dragons deep beneath.

Perihelion of the cicada through the brassy
July sky, schemata of blue pepsis wasp
vectors. An orange patch of sun
in the evening forest. Muffled symphonies
in the night traffic. Sand flats beside
the river under budding thickets
of staghorn sumac, high-water nests
in their boughs. Extension drift
on the Tethys ocean. The sound of far
waves. Sibilance of rain tires on the evening
bridge. Fierce array of the spring foliage,
we are strange progeny of three billion
years of solar irradiation. All details
threshold the effect.

Only the blue megahertz evening stars
ascending over the garden wall. Night
unfolds like no other inside her vagina.
Lust flowing sustained by her looking.
The eventide ascending high-rise moon
to White Sands. Streamline yourself
into the truth. The nighthawks emerge
from their hangars. The sun renewed
within itself decreed our prodigious
evolution.

A warm grey day in August. Beneath
the trees patches of night oscillate

with powdery luminescence. Nocturnal
pools characterized by crickets and day-
foraging bats. A wind stirs the fissures
of the canopy. What is still is expectant.
A distant blue-jay sounds the interceding
forest. Albino fox across the cedar verge.
Waves on Lake Huron. In your sleep
they are waves within breathing. The beach
absorbs remote momentums. Surges linger
in dreams a phantasmic waveform.
Her children, the lake claimed by dreaming,
lay waste the armoured spinal cord.
A delirious rush of invertebrate orgasms
in the implacable recall of the ocean.
Free-fall under the swells a pulsing spinal
thrill, diving to the source of neural
conductivity. Ammonite's copper mist
gleaming dully through the shallows.
Peripheral glimpse of trilobites scuttling
into murky water at the edge
of the Ausable. Hungry Hollow Hills,
memory vapour.

Deafening cicadas.

Fierce array of the summer foliage.

Re-group at the air-lock. Her spine ends
in four extra vertebrae, prehensile
as a finger. Her parents obviously intrigued
by the sexual options in the genetic

engineering catalogue. She has slight webs
between her fingers. The limestone heaves
up and dissolves in an awesome rumbling,
releasing the time trapped in its layers.
Legions of extinct creatures crawl out
of the rubble, transparent with age.
The planets converge and hover just
beyond the atmosphere in the evening sky.
Impossibly huge pastel spheres barely
opaque through the haze. Electromagnetic
fields spawn huge scarab beetles. Iridescent
armour and fabulous horns. Cascade
of night and night-wind coming
in the living-room window drugged
and cool. Full moon. Only the brightest
stars visible. I have learned to love
the noctuid moths.

Cumulonimbus clouds tower, their bases
below the horizon. Pink in the gasoline
haze and slanting rays of the setting sun.
Billowing like the convoluted foreheads
of brooding foetuses, their water-brains
filled with grotesque electric thought
impulses and thunder. Their silence
raining onto the land.

A consensual domain in the unrelenting
hunger of her mouths, glistening
lacunae in a tactile confluence of desire.
Merely her proximity. Faint blue lace-work
of veins beneath the lactose silk of her
breasts. Multi-foliate her orgasms
an interlocking network of pure sensual
detail rippling through the surrounding
forest. Giant silk moths in vibrating
clusters, wings still unfolding, still damp
with emergence. Electric gradients
in the anticipation zone of her touching.
Sunset glitters in the windows
of the planetarium.

Full summer moon rising obliquely over
the pitcher plants and miniature sphagnum
landscapes. Vigilance. Panavistic crystal
night-vision of the silver lynx, silhouetted
for an instant against the ocellus
of the summer moon. Hypnotic cameo
resumed without juncture. Stars drip
from the points of mulluscoid teats.

There can be no highlights if there is no
point of view. No reflections, no rainbows.
The virtual image is subject dependent.

Evening stars pealing off like no other.
Velvet theatre curtains undulate slowly
in the night wind, their lower folds wet

with pond water. Far red glow of smelters
and factories to the north. Hydrogen
pumps. Glacial clay bluffs and narrow
pebble beach of Tyrconnell. A mathematical
plain in critical grey light while Cenozoic
bivalves forage under the waves. Runaway
crouches in the amphibious June musk
of the peat-bog. Heat-wave sun vibrato
warms the moist forest floor, naked feet
on spongy humus, exotic insects splash
sudden erratic trajectories over the path.
Linnaeus a certain key.

Blue fluid support of summer sky eggshell
into evening explorations of sexual forests,
hot naked waists an intangible barrier
realizing the planet's dream. Green leaf
haze of April branches. An image without
recognition equal to the total configuration
surrounding her. The forest is alive
with itself, vegetable leather leaves
of the rhododendron. Behind manifestation
is manifestation. Slim curve of her waist
projected through the plane of symmetry.
Her pelvis vaulted like angel wings
just barely surfacing in the smooth
tautology of her hips. Her come-spangled
down. Drops of semen deliquesce
in the naked morning spectra. Her aureoles
glazed and wrinkled. Within the forest
a vapour resounds.

Nomenclature of rivulets, the dense
and kinematic vegetation of the windy
valley. Coal-swamp dusk in advance
of the evening terminator line. Mute and
recoiled September is a nation of secret
pacts. Summerhill, bleached grass
and a lone hawthorn tree halfway against
the late afternoon Polaroid receding blue
sky. Giant hairy fiddleheads of the tree
ferns. Nighthawks beckon from the bluff
of the line storm. Norse gold forged
in orgasms and sun, her face vigilant
in the first humid cobalt June storm wind.
Summer copper dusted pale green.
She runs the palm of her right hand
lightly over her left breast, her nipples erect
ozone the wind soft thunder in our ears.

There is no season uncorrupt of another.
Soft tropical storm at night in our
breathing. In the heart of fall there
is a summer glen. Evening cicadas. Heat
storm. White violet lightning flickering
sudden silhouettes, the frozen forest
staggered omnidirectional. Sassafras grove
in the ravine incalculable. A breeze
occasionally divulging the blue eggshell
evening. Raccoons awaken on oak
branches, heat wave somnolence their
masked regard. Wild grape vines. Dark
coils draped in the lower branches.

Constant gushing thrill the night
permeated. Eyes, ears, mouth, nostrils,
genitals, hands and feet. A night unmoved
by crickets until dawn. Red haven. Free
stone. Midnight in the hyper-personal
theatre of an August moon. Its reflection
in the lake an electric mirage loomed
a dazzling monotonous dream light.
The water quick molecular sand.

Ascend and merge.

Sunny harpsichord forest morning
blending imperceptibly into afternoon.
Night the Cenozoic asylum. All mammals
quickened in the autumn, their organisms
burning more fiercely. The glass machinery
intact as if an overlay filled equally
with allusion. The music stripped pure
of association. A heart igniting bittersweet
the dreams surrounding it. As if paradise
renewed a tangible and immaculate
perception. The fall from grace
is the remove itself. Caught in the first fine
figments of ice on the October pond.
An ice pavillion deep in the autumn forest,
skating down cool summer department
corridors of green and red. Ancient

summer snakes, Don and Humber wild
fingers deep into the city. Silver mist
audio-fog, an electronic grey day over Lake
Huron. Anticipation-slicked water lapping
Devon beaches. Glistening conglomerate
of the pebble incline. Eleuthera blue.
Weird music of the stars, raining down
upon all of this.

We have always made love this way, down
through all the ages. Archaeopteryx
glittering to the surface of the lithographic
stone. Distant amphetamine sex. A white
apartment building in the blue summer
night. The moon. A woman waiting
up there. Empty sunlight building. End
of the sparkling fjord. A stonehouse
chiaroscuro of yellow leaves, the sun torn
Polaroid blue and white Lawren Harris.
Mysterious aerials, their red lights glowing
in the coastal twilight. Mood beacons
of inexplicable childhood memories.
The orchestra suddenly quiet.

The summers that were and the summers
that never were.

Words from silence hatched, and its surface
glistening with paraboloids.

The night sand cold on top, warm

beneath. Ultra-violet dimly through
the tree ferns. The scenery strobes slightly
under the hot overcast swamp vision.
Limestone outcrops. Dew-drunk cecropia
moths aimlessly copulating with flowers,
twigs and fingers. Perfect sinusoid
of muscular flesh burning pink and blue
and orange. Unnatural grace of her moving.
Her urgent and delicate choreography.
Silk and gold. Leaves sliding long taut
abdominal trails across the skin palace
warm devon cream. Darkly traced
in a silence our vision does not seam.

There is a second order of darkness
rarely seen. Brick walls radiate tangible
heat at midnight. Tiny black rivulets
of road tar congeal in diminutive lava
flows. Lithographic stone, the miniature
jungle of a summer lawn. Distant FM Satie
on deserted night terraces. Calibrations
returning from a starry pasture.

Her tendrils alarming hyperbolas
in the dim atmospheric envelope.
Embryology. Insect résumé presumed
the manifest diode resplendent. Wind
a cheering shield of leaves, flickering

shadows on the light grey beech trunks
beneath. Buttressed against the observer's
opaque logo, this island is arraigned
through the visual scan of a hover fly.
The expressway burnt amber shimmering
with thermal inversion puddles. Staggered
grace the thin metal of rain on the pond's
surface.

Hum of huge electric engines and factories
on the horizon. The trees, straining
in terror, almost achieve visible movement.
The impossible children's valleys crumble
through backyards and living-rooms. Lips
drawn over the teeth in rictal fear
of the words being formed.

Down the axis of vision the angel
of revelation descends. When her eyes
close, the nocturnal annunciation will
begin. A single star over the attenuated
autumn foliage. Herald of the anti-dawn.
Delta of Venus fore-winged with vernal
espionage and silver. The perfect fossil
of an unknown species that will never
be found. The lions and unicorns
we wish to speak through.

PART 3
Concordat
Proviso Ascendant
(1981–1988)

She is beyond you now. Her piscine
features embryonic and dissipated
with wisdom. Her nakedness possessed
each time a seething harlequin of erectile
sequins. Her lips aching with honey.
The sky darkening with dreams.

There is a language to predicate
the adoration.

And the water, its essence an alarming
grace surging past the edge of your control.
Breeding miraculous witness. Command
spillover. Sunset blue spruce shimmer
vaguely, their translucent pagodas rising
like glass temples in the dusk.
The ammonoid's nacreous lustre, iridescent
stage lights in a Cretaceous theatre. Slow-
motion August trees, the Huron clay bluffs
blue in the lake haze and at night the stars
rain glittering onto the beach. Pyritized
mother-of-pearl a refraction so ancient
the dreams are blackened. This most
Devonian of raptures. A vowel away
from the discrete crystals in which her rude
beauty gives way to angels. As the planet
turns into the photon irradiation of dawn.
Our debt to the truth.

Beneath the lake a room. The water
electric. The smallest ripple transmitted

undiminished through the whole.
For its membrane is the source
of the cellular envelope, budding
cauldrons at the base of the falls.
It is living. It whispers and moans
a thousand voices inside the rapids.
It is the medium of choice for internal
predators.

Daylilies waxen cups of orange and red
conspiring under the late afternoon sun.
Dazzling cellular lattice. Rattlesnake Point.

Dusty milkweeds at the roadside. Summer
cricket fields phasing a pointillistic audio
plane. Waves of wind transparent molasses
in the leaves. Insect voyeurs.

It is night and there is a yearning
in the wind. Your heart a dusky corporeal
fragrance streaming into the stars.
In the moonlight you can see
the underwater trees. Devonian ocean floor
commands the summer sky a fossil sea.
Spicebush, oak and sassafras. The mouth
of the Ausable. Blue evening dunes
of the Pinery. This sunrise a coral fire
through the hardwood crowns. Leafless
spring forest glowing tide against the sun-
fissured escarpment. Incremental heat
of the vernal arc high over Collingwood.

Specific mist of August, pink and gold.
A morning light all day. The forest shade
almost colloidal, deepening under
the looming thunderheads. Lilacs.
Nicotinia. A penetrating dampness, limp
clothes and paper, the subway floors sweat
under her sandals. Gamelan the thrill
of her hands. A proton decay detection
chamber under the south shore of lake
Erie. Her toes almost a Fibonacci sequence,
her lips tasting of unknown cities. Rain
shimmers in the Zildjian forest. A bat
flying through Allen Gardens. Glass
membrane ruptured into the June night
sky, itself an infernal mosaic of irregular
cobalt tiles, prismatic sparks
at their interstices. Her sex flushed
by the fire lithe under the trees. Words
unable me to speak to you. There is a path
for you hear if you see it. Blue the colour
of opium once in a dream.

Awkward mammalian blossoms in lucid
sunlight the memory of a childhood
not our own. Occidental blue of April
afternoons, the far north an aerial clarion
in the heavens. As if the sky would coalesce
and reveal another scale of perspective,

a giant immanence of dreams born
in wordless childhood musings.
The April plainness of building materials
on cold grey afternoons. Provisional
shelter. At night the glistening celestial
machinery. Sky deepening with stars,
crescent of the new moon just setting
above the glow of sunset. Concrete
technical reality. There is a heraldry
in creation unseen. Stony morning brook,
sparkling water beads an optical essence
of the previous night's stars. Star dew.
The rain we pray for. Recognition
in the May foliage, secret arboreal house
of dreams and wind. Star corridors.
The axis insatiable. Labialithe.

A temporal music, each successive note
justified by its predecessor. Such subtle
harmony that the edge of dissonance
suspends the moment of recognition. Grey
and gold escarpment the October rain. Let
them all see it. May night reality of precise
darkness gushing the wildest hot metals
into her red-shift depths. Bronze rivers
sinuous with age. Boreal rawness of early
June foliage. Huron palisade the plateau
forest of the Escarpment. A single firefly,
portentous intermittent star wending
through dim canyons of spruce.
Meandering green ember insinuates

the solid obsidian glass night,
a supernumerary planet addir g strange
light to the stars. Unearthly m achinery
of the forest darkness. Nightshade. Low
frequency rumble at the planetary surface.
Summer sun a cool furnace in the furthest
depths of the moon. Solstice moon waxing
transluscent in the afternoon sky. Evergreen.
Chlorophyll and haemoglobin. Red Haven.
The music frightening and joyous.
I have the vehicle to take you there,
its gleaming fuselage a landscape
foreshortened by velocity.

Take command of the senses. You are all
that you see. Cardinal in the redbud.
The lake milky blue-green under the purple
sky of an approaching electrical storm.
Something ironic in you which is not fully
formed. This moment gone too far.
Delirium in the summer wind. Midnight
cicada. The horizon a window
of impossible perspective, multi-layered
stratus and cumulonimbus. Decalcomania
of deciduous clouds. A path the least
resistance.

Cap and talus of the Escarpment
diminishing into perspective haze
at our sides. Grimsby canyon an irresistible
ravine swift with gravity, sensual vapour

over the unwavering creek. Her abdomen
pale cream curdled with muscles. Her power
a private delight arched and supple.
Her thrall of nakedness. Pseudoscorpions
under shoes on the landing. Fruitflies.
Peaches. October moon a glaucous eye
through alto-stratus. A life refined to one
unbearable moment. Love a semantics you
invent between. Her touch a thrilling
cellular wind racing through my nervous
system. This wet skin and sweet absence.
The mild labile hysteria of gulls.

Lustful engine of summer metal incubating
in the late March railway soil. Hot shaft
of the vernal axis naked under bare sumac
branches. Her breath exquisite musk
reminiscent of the osmoderma. Elora
Gorge, summer reptile sunbanks
the aromatic morning cedar forest aloft
on each side. Ocular water sliding lager
beneath quick ledges. Limestone caves.
There is an ineffable music that lingers
in the charged air over the rapids. A single
note triggers intangible symphonies,
their strange harmonies blend
into the fabric of all sound.

L ate night rhapsody of the ecliptic,
ultramarine spangled with planets.
The looming, almost frightening wisdom
of children. The still city a crystal lattice
dreaming under the ghost shoals of glacial
Lake Iroquois. Our orgasm an embodied
mutual description. River mist pungent
malt of liquid leaves. Branches, roots,
boulders and niches, the landscape proffers
itself for our progress on the slopes.
Seminal blue electric glow within
the waterfall. Demerara floor of the cedar
forest. Limestone terraces mark the descent
of an ancestral river. Ramparts encased
in cedar foliage, a photon greenhouse
evanescent in July heat. Each bank
of the gorge an interior unknowable
to the other.

Darkness comes early in the valley, twisting
along the paths like warm river wind,
a corporeal zephyr. Time skewed
with silence in the chiming afternoon.
An autumn indistinguishable
from morning proceeding like no other.
The gorge sweats above the white heat
of the rapids. Cedar, hemlock, white pine
and birch. Elm and ash beyond. Gorge
patrol. Dry riverbed of twilight and night
in the cedar forest, fragrant darkness spills
down the shallow fossil valley.

Toronto interglacial overcast. A temperate,
deciduous freshwater marine light. Metal
at high speed. White clay bluffs
and summer interiors burgundy and light
dusty green. Purple stone. Wood smoke
and evening mist the water pellucid jelly.
Moiré of ripples an inverse solution
to the equation of shoreline. The wind
a sudden aerial rapids in the leaves.
This nightriver, gentle grade and bowl
and groove.

Faintly pungent, acrid limestone river rank
from trickle falls luxurious with moss.
Mercurial chipmunks, warm tubular
and insistent, their lingering stripes. Blue
ash. The forest roots a semiology we barely
comprehend. I have the music to take you
there, its gleaming fuselage just beyond
the curve of this hill. Drone of cicadas
adorning the beech temple, serpentine
roots burst the foundation stones.
Underwater shelves of limestone.
Salamanders moist beneath dry forest
rocks. Quantum flight of a hoverfly. Heavy
air, thunder low in the distance
as the elastic twang of a bullfrog locates
the shallows. The night gorge pulsing
with fireflies, moonlight on waves.
Trembling mica electron thunder
an underground city.

She is liquid darkness occult with desire.
Scattered curls of corrugated steel litter
the floor of an abandoned airplane hangar.
Eclipse sunlight, lancing through holes
in the roof, scatters perfect solar crescents
on the concrete. The naked air electric
we unite glistening in the light from giant
atmospheric machines rising above
the horizon. The sky filled with sound,
furious insistent joy as she cries, aching
chorus of electroluminescent orgasm. Heat-
bleached August fields. Cool green lawns
under humid tree caverns. Lambton forest
a cool sensual intuition, earthen paths
packed and powdered. Night perfume
of the magnolia blossoms drifting through
limestone trestles under the railway bridge.
Cicadas shimmer in the late summer trees.
Storm flooded city streets and aromatic
twigs. Her incendiary hands stoke
the September heat wave, a single katydid
rasping from the silver maple at midnight.
In the humid wind magnified leaf shadows
enact a restless cinema noir under
the backyard floodlight. Wild grapes
purple on the vine. Particulate smoky blue
haze of hot October afternoons. Indian
summer in the Berkshires. Manhattan.

Wild rhododendrons of the Hudson valley.

Becoming myself, I have become someone
else. My adoration the natural fulfillment
of her sacral narcissism. She is Eros
displayed. Lank salience of her thighs.
She drew a shade of stratus. Chunks
of stone erode into Mayan friezes. Gold
scarabs at Clark Point. Creek newts frankly
relaxed in the sandy aquarium delta
foliage. An otter near the forks of the Ervin
and Grand. Cedar roots dowsing Silurian
strata. Rococco acrobatics of cliff swallows.
She is here now. Her face a dark lantern
blossoming in the twilight. Every path
the most expedient solution of opposite
destinations. She lies down amongst
the ferns. Manitoulin cecropias. A flute
lost in the sound of rapids.

Scarab grubs harboured in scrub oaks.
We merge in the windy forest, in the rushing
neo-silence of a hot August wind,
in the mute aqueous clamour of leaves
under the wild hush. Our clothes sullen
layers of skin. Our giant bodies' moist
electric surfaces continuous with the forest.
Close upon us now this afternoon
an atmosphere of flesh. The smell of rain
on the wind. August hypnotized
in the chill depths of the lake. Mudpuppy.

Hellbender. September heat wave stone
temple haze along the beach distant signal
fires glimmering orange. Her water broke
the slow fall of evening leaves, waves
of silver-green above human creatures
coupling wondrous beneath. Chlorophyll
mist. The sky ringing with our music.

Our path a dark sweetness, musky tribute
to your consent. Your face miraculous
stone sweating in the August heat. The sky
a dream of cirrus and aquamarine, purple
silhouettes of distant airplanes descending
into the edge of night. High evening
this secret joyous darkness internally
illuminated by a fossil sun. Night windows
of a large home near the river. In the cool
twilight of the basement nocturnal children
interlock within the necessities of desire.
Their faces animal-flowers insensate
with beauty. Tropical leaf theatre under
stadium lights.

The stars through hot leaves, our bodies
dusted and engaged by a slender path.
Indistinct in twilight we slide into each
other. We ache for the river music, a blanket
of silence. Its impassive interior a mute

concourse. Night eyes. We are intruders
in our own house, incandescent lights
a peripheral flicker our bodies smudged
with soil. Our reflection in the picture
window, night trees behind. You come
rubbing against me. We come androgynous.
We come as two boys and then as two
women. A cistern of rainwater in the cellar,
a rainbarrel in the garden,
and in the stream our bodies merge
with warm river currents. Gradual
accumulation of insects at the porch light,
a glittering raiment. Our bodies quick
and light through the night air. Dusty pink
evening at the botanical gardens. Neural
storms in her pupils. A magnetic field
suddenly explicit around two trees
as a flock of birds erupting from one
is sucked into another like a solar flare.
Avian prominence the lines of force.
There are salamanders nearby.

Gothic geometry of the lycopod forest.
The axes of symmetry explicit
in the fern-crowns' angular lattice. Rustling
flight of a giant dragonfly. Its cellophane
wings glint in the Carboniferous sunlight,
a vanishing, airy chain of after-images.

The humidity of the gorge forest is higher
than the surrounding area. A world millions
of years in the past. Snake Doctor,
helicopter, red Doppler Shift. My camp
a rainforest vigil here at the transition zone.
The camouflaged wings of the moth
are pure representation. A path is an inter-
species collaboration. Distant rumble
of thunder, older even than shark.
Iridescent blue scarab deep within
the petals of a rose.

Watersnakes bask on sunny riverbanks.
Ion shadow of the thunderhead hovering
sightless over this forest a charmed garden.
Fabric of reality parting slightly just before
the lightning. Swimming naked
in the warm night river. Umbilical tornado.
Copper oxide and limestone chambers.
Lynx rampant on a field sable. Crown
of night. The margin of heaven and earth
blurred this evening. Moonrise.

The water is continuous music manifesting
the bias of the valley. Adolescents shimmer
in the corruption of self-consciousness,
their limbs bronze and gold under
the summer sun. The forest a cathedral,
its floor studded with remains of ancient
temples dedicated to unknown gods. Elora
gorge an erogenous wound in the surface

of the limestone. Dusky salamanders,
translucent licorice speckled with silver.
There is a landscape that corresponds
to each station of the heart, a geography
for every phase of our lives.

The gorge is a rift valley in time,
an amphitheatre of cedar and limestone.
Hot green twilight of the forest depths.
Decaying Hindu temples, each built
on the crumbling summit of its predecessor.
Roots and vines form a twisted webbing
over limestone walls. Umbrella magnolias
and blue ash. Giant swallowtail butterfly
momentary cadmium in the shadowy
interior of the forest. Water wrestling
with rocks in the depths of the rapids.
The air in the gorge still and heavy,
the sky misting over into a featureless
bright grey haze, maximum heat of early
evening. Remote thunder. Nighthawks,
crickets, bats and raccoons, unbroken
wild continuum into the centres
of the great-lake cities.

Karst topography. Bright hypnotic
splendour of the solstice noon.
A dragonfly lands on her shoulder,

its opalescent wings glitter in the June
sunlight. Endless summer night of the high
Arctic Eocene. Her ancestral Devonian arms.
Giant catalpa trees bear signal standards
of white blossoms. On still nights
their fragrance cascades in sweet penumbras,
nocturnal skirts of perfume. Limestone
trestles of the railway bridge are erotic
monuments in the television foliage
of an industrial-age summer. Barberry
blossoms' spermy pungence on hot June
nights. Cartilaginous sex. Grey diffuse light
of memory, a sensualizing texture irrupting
and sweetening everything with cosmic
nostalgia for the moment. Each second
a prodigal return, reality affirmed
with recognition.

Fess engrailed. Mammatocumulus lit
from beneath by the setting sun. Night
hardwood on the summer campus,
Corinthian columns ascend through
successive tiers of concentric leaf mobiles,
deciduous candelabra. Their outlines slowly
ripple in the hallucinogenic mist
of this nocturnal forest, indiscernible
from the faint animation of the night wind.
Delicate wallpaper clouds slide across
the full moon in this blue cinema night.
The forest is a room we blend into. Involute
masters of uncertain dimensions.

Muscular black night wind. Dry summer
wind dusty with stars. Blowing clear
and hot from the boreal summer.
Jerusalem sirocco through northern valleys,
dark mountains stir inside the alchemical
night, giant sensual gods cast in basalt.
Desert wind a thousand years old and clear
as deuterium pools, a wind blowing empty
through our hearts, their mysterious
longing. A wind that pulls us wordless
from our bodies, the rushing final wind.
The historical wind erotic and devout,
stone deities coupling on the walls
of jungle temples. Eocene nachtmusik.

So fair our green. Testicular sacs
of the oriole nest, winged persimmons
in her green vigilance. The honeysuckle's
buzzing insect aura. Sun sporadically
through hazy cumulus clouds, the lake
impenetrable with mist. Stiff, incremental
surge of growing trees. Forest light
is the perpetual, internal twilight of dreams.
I am the fisher king of my unconscious.
Root cascades on rocks, gnarled retainers
for terraced humus waterfalls, re-enactment
of a fossil rapids. Marvellously uneven
terrain. Forest rocks luminous
with condensation, green antler-velvet
congealed into stone. The clamour
of the storm lags in noisy streams.

Distant apartment complexes become
moody empires of light, subdued
orange constellations in the twilight haze.
Revelation of the rainy day. Late night
resurrection of a forgotten love, a vanished
civilization where the waning moon
is the accusatory eye of an abandoned
lover. Metaphysics in dusty light
on the trunks of the Norway Spruce, cicada
husks at their bases. Windbreak colonnade.
Love's absence is love still, the heart
a celestial wound. August a certain Aegean
light through us all. The beach
a commotion of light and waves, cries
of gulls and children blend in the wind.
Honeysuckle vines redolent of evening,
a dusky corona of ruby throats. Surprising
articulation of children's backs,
their advanced hominid wisdom. Wild
cherry gum on raw copper. The dull gleam
of tin roofs. Field of hydroelectric power
flickering in the darkness at the bottom
of the lake.

She is delightfully augmented.
In the distance vandals break the windows
of a deserted factory, disembodied locus
of fear. Meander. She walks almost

laboriously around her endowments,
a libidinous and circuitous elegance.
She is crippled with sex, ripe fruit
on a slender bough. Resume the broken
discourse of the gods. Quick vertigo of lust.
The milky way wheeling on the axis
of an immense black hole through
abandoned zodiacs in the mysterious
depths of an intergalactic summer night.
A continuous indoor atmosphere extends
uniform and infinite in all directions.

PART 4
Time Wind
(1989–1997)

Coal forests of the Carboniferous delta
swamps. Lepidodendron trees,
their anthracite trunks embossed with spirals
of interlocking diamond leaf-scars. Exquisite
fusain sceptres. Snakes and ladders.
The river current quickens as it nears
the falls. Elastic water pulled viscous
over the lip. Fossil glen. *Nine Dragon Scroll*
evening above Lake Erie. The forest rises
in music like an ancient air. Twilight
priestess administers the evening,
her dark splendour.

Entrance colonnade to the oak forest,
micro-climate of hardwood shade
an emerald nave. Distant figures numinous
through summer haze. Windy August stars
drift over sighing pine trees. Pine-grove star
needles. When we come it rains. Indexed
by sassafras trees the grassy hills undulate
with soft Miocene turbulence in the July
heat. High summer. Giant bulrushes. Night
herons motionless on terrapin logs.
An insect alights momentarily on a stainless
steel stela. Luminous dream vista.

Pipes, water mains, gas lines – the roots
of houses spread under the landscape.
Sandy paths. Calm, alert valley air. Muted
tinkle of lawn parties beside smoky
rhododendrons. Honey locusts shelter

summer in their green October foliage.
Cool July day, her long, honeyed thighs
slipping out of her jeans as she crouches
to pee in the forest loam. Fine pale arches
of her feet, the hot gush of her. March
hills – secret blue drifts of snow
in sheltered hollows on the northern
slopes. Glacial refugia.

Redtail oak forest. Narcissistic talisman
of our love. A metallic green haze between
the columns of this metropolitan forest –
lovers wet with lust. Ginkgo leaves. August
tea roses, pink, orange and cream.
The constant, almost inaudible rustling
of leaf mulch on warm nights in early
spring. Soil and leaves heaving
in slow-motion turmoil as dew-worms slide
through autumnal debris – a faint,
chalky crinkling.

June empire of green, a coronation
of green. Aquamarine and jasper. Blue-
green. Yellow-green. Green of constancy
and desire. Corundum. Verdigris streaks
on limestone walls.

Hot, still air. Heat waves linger in closed
rooms. Unfortunate your beauty.
Disastrous your lovely salamander arms
beside the restaurant patio hedge. The city
is a ripple-tank of violet and orange, hot
steel pounded into the shapes of machines.
The simple, rude pragmatism of size.
Intolerable heat of a single desk lamp
as moths gather at the window screen.
River-musk smell of dried algae. Luscious,
earthen scent of cantaloupes and peaches
in a wooden bowl on the kitchen table.
Tickets till dawn. Spring twigs,
their buds reptilian, as we are reptilian
in our extremities. Scaled and cool
the clear borders of my own partiality.

The Cliffbrake fern's blue-green tenacious
filigree. Niagara-on-the-Lake twinkling
in the stone night. Hot July afternoon.
Deserted apartment buildings. An extinct
river reconstituted in the meandering
course of the willow brake. The children
who play inside. Green tissue commotion
as a praying mantis rises laboriously
through the August mist under a sodium
vapour lamp. Indistinct conversation
of restaurant patrons leaving the patio
in small groups. Giant silk moth. Unseen
river sliding noiselessly behind all this.

Blue midnight sky behind deserted
buildings. Nostalgia steeped in its own
intoxication. Empty dance pavilion
beneath the summer stars. Every forest
is a beckoning sensual labyrinth of lust.
Radiowave rooms echoing within rooms,
the hollowness of love remembered
within love realized. The lonely bliss
of completion. Delicious emptiness
in this late summer night. After
the dance a waning moon rises. We walk
through vacant streets past buildings
filled with sleepers. Their dreams
perfuse the night air.

Tonight the sky is inky black, a carbon
night without a trace of blue behind
the full moon. It is a deeper evening,
a universe slightly more vacant
than before, as if this warm darkness
required a triumph of representation,
as if the sky conformed to its own
description in a continuous devoted hue.
A single cricket calls from the grass beside
the barn. Indigo summer.

Purple and grey. Metallic dust
in the subway tunnels. Darkness

at the interstices of the city. Burgundy
on limestone. Lilacs bending in a rainy
wind. University residences glowing deep
yellow. The airport thundering through
the night air. Wind in the Wychwood oaks.
Green argon lasers flicker over Queen
street sidewalks. Dirigibles. Asphalt
lagoons. A nightflight banks above
the spreading ledges of city lights.
The streets are vast crystalline networks,
linked luminescent organisms proliferating
to the horizon. Cooling lava glowing
through a lacework of cracks. Moonlight
on lake Ontario a dazzling path
to the dawn.

Fireworks explode in the summer night.
Pyrotechnic blossoms of silver and gold.
Their dazzling, empty perfection. Spring
aches within a palace deep inside
the autumn forest. A clear evening
with celestial gauze so that the largest stars
have misty haloes. Jupiter, Mars
and Venus. I know you are love,
in the absorbent summer twilight
of the forest strand.

Enigmatic nocturnal waves phosphoresce

on the moonlit shore of an inland ocean.
Beech trunks incarnate with cloud light,
as if you weren't sure you were naked
in a dream. Moccasin flowers. Trilliums.
Lightning blossoming in the purple strata
of distant storms. Wild grapevines spill
from the branches of white oaks
overhanging the creek. A suffusion
of emerald light through the waist-high
ferns, our clothes soaked with rain
and sweat.

We follow the river down the Escarpment
ravine. The clouds a violet-grey ceiling
to this vast, open-air greenhouse. The air
thick and hot, the foliage dripping
with recent rain. In the forest a deserted
building. Tiny furious engine of a hover fly
suspended in mid air. English ivy growing
behind storm windows, leaves pressed
green against the glass. Darting
and hovering, a flock of cedar waxwings
hunts insects at the edge of the marsh.

There is a darkness outside the city. Her
face vigilant through night elm corridors.
Summer lawn under green cumulus trees.
The city park full of couples. She resembles
herself darkly, like a sensual memory.
Her wrists exalting with such cruel delicacy
as always attends on beauty. Our hands

alive to each other. Exist, to quicken the air
around us, for this moment we are golden.
Red oaks. The night guides us. It is warm
outside and the air moves the leaves
variously. Her pelvis vaulted light. Powdery
with stars from a desert night, the wind
has come to blow what is weightless
in us away.

Dactyl leaves of the white oak.
The white-tailed deer are melanized
thermograms of themselves. A consensual
domain in the summer wasteland. Giant
Haida eyes stare from beech trunks,
their rapt bliss.

Lyrical monotony of the whip-poor-will's
song. Jupiter and Mars bright through
the lattice of oak leaves. This nightjar's
haunted clockwork call conjures memories
and floating reminiscences. Hollow music,
as if the soul were a cuttle-bone. Sinister
to be so bold. Mist over the river.
The whip-poor-will stops the night.

Multifoliate her orgasms curl and vanish
into the landscape. One pure interlocking
network of desire. Thought impulses

and thunder, my fingers water dispersing
porous into the land. Dwarf chinquapin
oak savannah of the Pinery dunes.
Black oak. A late cold spell decelerates
the unfolding spring foliage. Magnolia
flowers transfixed in perpetual blossom
for two weeks. Lilac and forsythia likewise
suspended in chilled vegetative orgasm.
Raw spring sun on tombstones. Granular
luminescence in the grass.

Naked, she places her foot on a limestone
boulder and reaches up into the leaves.
Rapture. And touching you my dreams lay
waste the foliage of your nervous system.
Soft electronic hiss of night wind
in the tree tops. Purple night of city rain.
Glowing video-jelly oozes drugged
and gelatinous from a slice
in the television cable – clear, iridescent
gum flickering with electric colours.
The rasping call of nighthawks through
an open window. Raccoon eyes glowing
red in our headlights. Leaf shadows.

Delicate precision of an albino fox.
Its white fur ruffled by the wind
before the storm. Umbrella magnolia
leaves amplify the sound of the first
raindrops. Cold-cream scent of linden
blossoms in early July. The eyespots

of the polyphemus moth are reminiscent
of an earlier civilization, of smooth
futurist caterpillars, their hallucinogenic
blue evening reverie both alien
and unconscious of itself. On the outskirts
of the city there is a forest.

A muddy river shines in the darkness
beneath the aquaduct. Rain falling all night.
Red cedars luminous with hundreds
of green diamonds in the flashlight beam.
The Bouguereau August light. Local time
anomaly, thrilling August mist over several
days. Darkness so that the night can see.
Waxy green gloss of oak leaves in July sun.
The forest rejoices at the sound of distant
waves. This choice conceived by her seeing.

Teetering flight of a butterfly,
its destination barely a probability.
Dwarf hackberry. Swamp white oak.
Hoary bats tumbling like acrobats
through the savannah airspace. Margin
of evening. Twilight congeals as the first
raccoons descend the chinquapin oak.
Hanging gardens, ceaselessly dark
at the bottom where grub-jewels glisten
in the hollow oak's loam.

On the grassy flats behind the dunes giant
cicada-killer wasps establish restless, uneasy
field colonies. Their magnetic, zig-zagging,
hovering flight, as if suspended
on the wobbling tips of fine metal rods.
Shagbark hickory and sycamore. Lights
twinkling on Kettle Point. The long curve
of the beach. Grand Bend on the Ausable.
August fireflies beside the evening river,
wandering fairy-lights.

The machinery stands poised
and glistening in the forest clearing.
Slow metallic grind of the morning's first
cicadas. August rising through fields
and forests, the height of summer.
The dust on the path an inlaid palimpsest
of shoe-tread geometries, a hieroglyphic
pastiche. We articulate every surface
with our insignia. This internal summer
a tender flood. Spiders are sinister optimists.
Red bats careen through the light-cones
of street lamps, their velocity gathered
outside the light's perimeter.

Late August gold, silvery haze and hot
wind in the trees. Swells of wind
in the grass, orange sunlight and a black
swallowtail butterfly. Goldenrod. The field
autumnal, dry. Limestone wind, damp
and humid. August where it was named.

August where it began.

All the invisible cameras shift into our eyes.
Deep in the light field of the city a pink
electric sky glows through the evening
foliage. Delicate rustling of leaves moving
in the wind. Them. Honey to the quick.
Spent hurricanes of late summer, flooded
culverts and drains. Giant sphinx moth
at the porch light. White sunlight, white
sand. All day on the beach. Cottonwood
fragrance in a hot lake wind. Calm bowls
of still air in the lee of the dunes. Tactile
revelation of stone bridges, the dream city.

Early June evening. Dark overcast sky
behind green leaves. Sexual green,
handsome green. Malachite. This summer
grey and startled. Our broken lives
illuminate it with such sad delight.
The world is ourselves come
to this childhood wisdom.

The flesh of the apple is a strategy,
the summer night sky a cathedral of stars.
In the coal swamp the lepidodendron trees
rise. Their helical blazonry of mysterious
bituminous crystal. Jet coal. Methane

from an ancient swamp suffusing
the depths of a coal mine. Giant
salamanders stir in the slurry
at the bottom of the elevator shaft.

Twilight deepens as the sky loads
its nightware. Bright tedium of the whip-
poor-will's call. Its empty, lonely song
a kind of memory entrapment. This night
connected to all nights. The whip-poor-
will's bubbling call receding into darkness.
Its carnal song an ominous invitation,
an absent counterpoint over the bleak,
modulated surge of distant diesel engines.

She is darkness enthralled, slender stem
of pink mist. Her delicate white metallic
night. The summer sun low and softly
stabbing the weird overture of the stars.
I have seen this day from the other side
of my life. Dusty green leaves of the silver
maple bending in the wind. This wind,
this light. All alone in the dream of night.
Arkona. The sound of a far horn.
Unknowable desire, unknowable wisdom.
A white subtropical forest hanging
in the air like a cipher of sound. Wind
gusting on a hot afternoon.

Limestone boulders rise from the depths
of the hills, eroding into fantastic shapes

as they surface. The soil is an ocean, a fluid
heavy with thousand-year viscosity. Blind
worm snakes. Tunnels, roots, and the smooth,
underground shapes of truffles. Mozart
from an open window in a country home.
Empty heraldry all the more profound
because it is unconscious. Sitar monotone
of high-tension wires humming above
the transformer station. May evenings
before the nighthawks arrive.
She is otherworldly, immediate.

Sunspots crackle through the radio waves.
The planets are caught in that higher music.
Aurora Borealis. Solar wind conjures
an iridescent crown on top of the world.
Sweet nocturnal fragrance of sycamore
foliage. Silver stars cast into the dark wells
of the sky. The wind a waterfall in the tree
tops. The marvellous machines waiting
silently in the forest clearing, starlight
gleaming on their polished metal contours.
Smoke tendrils rise from the smoldering
campfire, time uncoils in arabesques.

Sweet desert of soul spreading
into the city you *are* this still evening.
Andromeda galaxy overhead, a tiny, fuzzy
colossus. The night sky a time-mosaic.
Distant symphonies from the bandshell
in the park. Eocene light, Mesozoic light,
light from before the earth existed. Time
wind blowing through the Milky Way.
An evanescent stardust settles
on the flowers in the garden.

The night sky is prehistory factored
by the speed of light, a thick lens of time
jelly, photon molasses. The faintest stars
further back in time, the edge
of the universe is its beginning. The pure
retrospection of starlight, lamented light
from extinct suns and remote galaxies.
Countless stars that have shone
on forgotten cultures of unknowable
complexity. Lost technologies in the hard
silver twinkle at the shore of this pond.

A gold scarab waits deep within
the cottage dream. Clark Point.
In the river the green newts are kipped,
strewn by gnostic impulse in the sandy
shallows. Beside them, miniature
underwater mountainscapes of algae
and pond weed. A scarlet tanager streaks
through the green oaks. Limestone
pavement showing through bare patches
in the savannah. Moonlight inside a dark
October lake. Our strange, liquid intimacy
in this lush landscape. Thrill of moist
warm air in secret rooms, the velvet light.
Sex a delicious conspiracy focusing
the wisdom of the trees.

Clarion fountain above all this. Jazz
saxophone sliding languid over the pool
in smoky loops and tusks. Hypnotic music
of desire. The logic of indiscretion. Soft-
shelled terrapins slip into the water
at our approach. Late April storm and
lightning-sparkle saturates our peripheral
vision until our flesh flickers. We make
love in the rush of warm rain. Orgasm-
shivers flash neuronal like foxfire through
our single body. Thunder rupturing
the clouds overhead in wild, extraneous,
baritone ventriloquism. The rain splashing
on your long thighs. Goosebumps, rain-
foam pubic hair. Thunder rippling above,

murmuring like memory or revenge.
The grassfires of early April. Fortnight of dry
weather before the foliage humidity engages.

There is only one night, one day. The March
full moon the last high, winter moon. In April
the lunar arc is low in the southern sky,
a summer moon.

Outdoor concert in the park bandshell.
The empty stage lit up. The audience
a dark mammalian cobble of heads fading
into blackness beyond the footlights.
In summer our afternoons are bright
and cruel with youth. These our mouths,
our sex, are dark openings into mute
unknowable bliss. As if the city were a desert
and we were a people of prophecy. Spring
on the Forbidden Planet, dune reverie of lost
alien civilizations on warm moonlit evenings.
Blades of grass like narrow, supplicating
astronomers in the night wind. Realm
sensualist her gold mail and silk indispensible.
Midnight dew trickling down the sides
of the glass machinery.

The afternoon we fell through each other
into this magnificent autumn of fire

and ice. We haunt this season in a white
room, flickering ultraviolet light flooding
insubstantial through the architecture
of our skin. You are a leaf drifting to earth,
a thin, spiral galaxy. This sunny autumn
wind. The blue optical spruce.
You are worshipped in the emptiness
at the threshold of the temple.

Spring insists, in all its tragic splendour.
Crickets interrogate the night,
their insect Morse a sourceless gamelan.
Still summer evening, pink-gold sunset
over the viaduct trestles. Wish now
the train were upon us. Ultra-violet moon
in a purple sky. Together we are erotic
technicians. The exquisite panic of orgasm,
divine rush of electric honey flesh burning
the mind clear. The immanent hush
of pure existence, rapture in the grey
nineteen-eleven, industrial Victorian
landscape. Iroquois delirium of the sandy
red tobacco fields near Delhi. The Milky
Way high over the Huron dunes.

Middle Island. Sandusky Ohio. Neutral
rimsherds catch the evening sun
on the forest floor. This site continuously

inhabited since the mammoths. Smooth,
low-grade ecstasy of summer evenings –
soon giant moths and shining chestnut-
coloured beetles. Tornado music drifting
up the Thames Valley from Windsor.
Spencer Davis Group faintly on the windy
radio. Morning mist over the lily-pads,
zebra swallowtails weave pointillist
diagonal nets above the milkweed
blossoms.

Sitar drone of cicadas in the understory
of the coppice, hills covered with young
hardwoods. Brief stroboscopic flicker
of a bird's shadow. Pathless livingroom
forest of trunks, leaf-litter and patches
of sunlight beneath the leaves. Vultures
ride hot thermals over the crest
of the Escarpment.

Late nineteen-sixties basement rec-room,
wood-panelled summer trapped
in the September night forest. Summer
with walls, summer interiorized
by coolness and finiteness – intimate,
desperate summer. The faint scent
of skunk. Summer self-confident
and mortal riding maximal the dreams
of September. Summer like gimmick
mountain. Synthetic, autumnal summer.

Lust under the industrial floodlights.
Aromatic with new leaves and warm soil,
the night sky is a cavern filled with stars.
Dark emerald wind blowing through the trees.
We walk under the constellations
out onto the lawn. Oak Ridges Moraine
conceives ravines to the north. Layers
of brown lignite with lenses of carbonized
peat. Glassy vugs full of anthracite crystals.
Hibernating lung-fish sleeping
in their dried mucus sacs.
Their 300 million year exile.

In the twilight a giant sphinx hawkmoth
hovers among the nicotinia flowers,
its long, wiry tongue glinting
in the streetlight as it threads the necks
of the blossoms. Distant traffic
on the lakeshore expressway. Waning moon
rising like a stained memory, a maculate
reminiscence of its fullness. The evening
sunlight on these pink, finite flowers,
only once – eternal in the certainty
that this tableau will never be again.
An endless series of such moments, each
nesting a thousand inner moments. All lit by
this metallic, golden light.

In late March a comet effluoresces
at the zenith, its pale areolus like a cosmic
supernumerary nipple. The comet

an omen, an emissary of cool summer
darkness. Its eye is a soundless moaning
fetish, its tail a blown phosphorescent
aether, alarming smudge of infra-
moonlight. Tonight the comet
is an apostrophe of time in the night sky
while March mud congeals and freezes
under the trees. The comet a vanishing
spectral finger pointing with monotonous,
empty grace at the sun. Such silence,
such distant commotion.

Bibliography Of Creatures

AMPHIBIANS
Red Backed Salamander
Wood Frog
Mud Puppy
Common Tree Frog
Ornate Chorus Frog
Spring Peeper
Eastern Newt
Tiger Salamander

REPTILES
Green Snake
Hog-nosed Snake
Decay Snake
Milk Snake
Snapping Turtle
Five Lined Skink
Red Bellied Snake

INSECTS
All the Saturnidae moths,
Cecropia, Luna etc.
Blackwing Damselfly
Black Swallowtail
Firefly
Annual Cicada
Green Darner Dragonfly

Giant Swallowtail Butterfly
All the Scarabaeidae beetles,
June bugs, Dung beetles, etc.
Giant Sphinx Moth
Stag Beetle
Giant Water Beetle
Praying Mantis

MAMMALS AND MARSUPIALS
Pygmy Shrew
Deer Mouse
Big Brown Bat
Red and Hoary Bats
Lynx
Flying Squirrel
Fox
Mole
Opossum
Raccoon
Silver Haired Bat
Little Brown Bat

BIRDS
Great Horned Owl
Nighthawk
Sparrow Hawk
Great Blue Heron
Snowy Egret

Ruby Throated Hummingbird
All swallows
Cardinal
Mourning Dove
Whip-Poor-Will

WEATHER
Cool sunny days in April and late October
Electrical Storms
Tornadoes
Line storms
Humid heat waves
Grey days in August with warm gentle wind
Wind on full moon late in spring
Unusually warm weather in winter

PLANTS
All Ferns
Winter Broadleaf Evergreens (any)
Sundew
Tiger Lily
Day Lily
Honey Suckle
Lady's Slipper
Pitcher Plant
Rhubarb
Slime molds
Fescue

TREES
Paw-paw
Umbrella magnolia
Magnolia
Catalpa
Cedar
Chestnut
White elm
Gingko
Dawn Redwood
Sassafras
Beech
Tulip
Kentucky Coffee Tree
Spruce (Blue)
Ailanthus
Butternut
Chinquapin Oak
White Oak

PLACES
Rock Glen
Hungry Hollow
Kettle Point
Bayfield
Cambridge
Dundas
Royal Ontario Museum
Pelee Point

Niagara Escarpment
Paris
Kingston
Tyrconnel
The Coves
Ausable River
Elora Gorge
London
Rondeau
Stratford
Mount Nemo
Rattlesnake Point

GRID ERECTILE

Because of its erotic and cool underparts and the
   sunset emblazoned on its membranous back. Its
   electric litheness.
Because it is a living distillation of twilight.
Because it is large and soft with external gills.
Because it is tropical and changes colours.
Because the pattern on its back is a thin point.
Because they are so numerous and docile.
Because it whispers through foliage. An animate
   mobile tendril of chlorophyll.
Because it is like an adder, spawning mythology.
Because it is beautiful like a sleek girl with a choker.
For the milk sliding couples beaded with honey.
Because it is large and primitive and therefore closer
   to the dinosaurs.
Because they are the only lizards we have.
Because they fly around mercury vapour lamps at
   night and alight on suburban screens with their
   exotic and large bodies.
Because of their silent glittering black flight.
Because of a summer evening in nineteen-fifty-four.
   It opened its wings and I received its revelation.
Because of summer nights behind the mosque.
Because it signals the height of summer.
Because of its mathematical precision at the infinite
   disposal of curiosity.
Because it is a tropical species here in Southwestern
   Ontario.

Because they are nocturnal, tropical thin points of extreme beauty. Sculptural perfection in living and dense wood.

Because their chrysalis resembles a vase. Their humming flight and the insoluble intricacy of their June camouflage.

Because of the size and gothic modelling of their pincers, their chestnut brown wing covers.

Because it is so tiny. (Weighs as much as a dime.)

Because it is pale underneath. Tawny above.

Because it is the eyes of night.

Because it is even larger, like a fox bat.

Because it is our largest and only cat.

Because they are capricious night gliders.

Because it is a predator.

Because of its inky fur. Tunnels twisting around roots.

Because it is a southern species migrating northwards. Evidence for an inter-glacial warming trend.

Because of their glowing eyes in the driveway at night. Their rasping marsupial cries.

Because of the caves.

Because of its unearthly face.

Because it is all of night.

Because it is a falcon.

Because it is sub-tropical.

Because it is a stilted and accurate blue mist.

Because it is the south, unwarranted in an ox-bow pond.

Because it is a tropical species, slowly migrating north.

Because it is a sub-tropical iridescent metal.

Because they are astonishing aerialists.
Because the vacuum of space is so near.
Because of a dream.
Because they draw out the soul.
Anticipation. Charged gradients. The irresistible
approach the arc hammer. Excitation in the ion
shadows.
Because they come after you and seem to float in
dreams, the bend sinister.
Because of the storm.
Because of an erotic insularity in the moist almost
tropical wind.
Because they illuminate everything in a grey
powdery light and turn the outside into a surreal
theatre of marvellous intent.
The warmth allows the spectators to remove their
clothes.
Lunacy and a saturnalian trance of corporeal clarity.
Because they are tropical.
Because they are both out of place and welcome.
Because they witnessed extinct races of fabulous
creatures.
Because it is carnivorous and wet.
Because it is a carnivorous morning jewel in the
sphagnum.
Because they are full lips and vulvas and are all of
summer.
Because they are a tropical species here in
Southwestern Ontario.
Because it has huge leaves and is tropical with cerise
Jurassic fruit.

Because it is fragrant and tropical.
Because its fruits are pungent.
Because the flowers are huge. Night glowing and
   perfumed.
Because of the pools.
Because their smooth mahogany pebbles are enclosed
   in vegetable geodes.
Because of fovea centralis.
Because they flowered all of beneath into above and
   translated it perfectly.
Because it is a living fossil.
Because of the colour and smoothness of its bark,
   the silence and level loam floor of the beech forest.
Because of the fragrance of its gum.
Because of the wooden petals of their flowers.
Because of the waterfalls and the morning glen.
Because it is the memory capital of Canada.
Because I perceived an order there.
Because the concretions are there.
Because of mid-summer nights, memory steeped
   in fireflies.
Because it overlooks Lake Huron.
Because the cedar pools are nearby.
For it was once submerged.
Because it is a huge invisible river.
Because of the collections in the grey specular
   light of Toronto winter afternoons spent in the
   Devonian era.
Because it is semi-tropical and on the same latitude
   as California.
Because it is a cathedral of limestone.

Because it is awesome.
Because chronology was commenced there.
Because of the black river formation. Last hold-out
of the White Elm.
Because of the beech forest and what came after.
Because I got to know Lake Erie and glacial clay
there.
Because I grew up beside them and they taught me
everything I know.
Because it is a huge and silent underwater predator.
Because it is huge and primitive.
Because it cruises, hovering, long snouted
crocodilian.
Because it is primitive.

PERMUGENESIS

There is a second order of darkness
and lens of distance. Brick walls
radiating tangible heat at night flowering
in the inky strata of far storms. Limestone
corridors of stone above the miniature
jungle of a rainless summer day in hot
August. The fingers on vacant F.M. patios
at night a distant Fragonard brain coral.
Sun spotted from a starry pasture.

Her tendrils' alarming relationship to dawn
as the dim calculations of an envelope.
Insect résumé presumes the moon. Fall
witnesses resplendent. Wind a cheering
field of the moon. Buttressed against
the observer's opaque logos in the summer
spectrum each has arraigned. Staggered
grace the thin metal of rain
on an Ordovician lily pond. The hum
of huge electric engines and green copper
tubing. Luna moth distance. Clouds
of dust and cool forest pond, fading
into the dream's edge. Our voices dissolve,
some hand or shadow moving into the city.
Here at the panavistic surface lips
are drawn over teeth, a shadow moving
through the words being formed.

This is of two somnophilias, those
that descend down the line of vision
where lunar mottled eels stir the attenuated

autumn foliage. A distant star over both
these mechanisms. Delta their parts
with corresponding espionage and silver.
The glass declension a focal sphere
contracting around our summer carnality.
The perfect fossil of an unknown generates
itself with its own repetitive logic.

August a haze amniotic our darkness rarely
witnessed. The trees are sentinels
in the vicious midnight heat. Tiny black
sexual visions. The awesome rumbling lava
flows. Lithographic stone within grey
libraries dreaming the summer lawn. Satie.
Distant forest proceeds before us at night.
Calibrations returning leaves. Dolomite
temple walls rise from thermal inversion
puddles. Water leaving limestreaks
out of pale rain on the pond's surface.
Water droplets posing hyperbolas
in the dim atmospheric abacus.
A gravitational field résumé presumed
the manifest diode. Colour of light
these leaves absorbed, wind a cheering
shield of leaves. Witness this opaque
logos, this island of a hoverfly.
Here at the panavistic surface vacuum-
eyed marsupials file quickly, bathed
in a neocarboniferous glow. An infinite
part of an unknown species that will never
be repetitive enough to speak through.

Unnatural grace of an Ordovician lily
pond, trickling unrestrained into her urgent
green copper tubing. Luna moths' gold.
Leaves sliding long taut ponds, fading
into the dream's edge. Skin palace cool
devon cream, our voices dissolve, some
hand or shadow our eyes do not seam.
Thick spurting shadow moving
through the words. Unnatural
choreography of her silken palace.

Triassic afternoons blending
imperceptibly into early forest morning.
Each huge spring bud a transparent
Cenozoic asylum. All mammals quickened,
wings unfolding into bats. Every organism
burning more fiercely. Distant radar
tunnels. The glass machinery intact
as remoras vacuous and cold that lurk
in hearts burning bittersweet dreams.
The air is water. The skin, neither moist
nor dry from grace is the remove itself.
Caught dividing the summer landscape
into figments of ice on the October pond.
An ice heart and stomach, the surfacing
of autumn forest, skating down cool
summer corridors of green and red.
There is a darkness outside of the city.

Anticipation slicked our own hearts.
The source a distant thunder in a weird
remote control music of the stars, raining
intrusions of stone within sky. Rumblings
from the earth made love like this. Down
through all the land breaking like ice,
glittering at the surface of the familiar
woman. Glacial amphetamine
lovemaking. A white on the plants,
and on the musicians, their blue summer
night. A woman gazes at the Polaroid
chiaroscuro of yellow leaves, the sun torn
on plants. Mysterious ariels, their events
accumulate through time in the coastal
twilight. Mood beacons of the Silurian
beach, no plants, little oxygen, childhood
memories. Greenway park, pebbles
of edible beige that were and the summers
that never were.

The fall from grace is a permeable
membrane of cells, the first fine figments
of ice on the pink and blues. Spring aches
in a palace deep in the autumn forest.
Skating men in moist soil and moonlight,
department corridors of green and red.
Don and Humber wild fingers into those
confined to light. The night sand cool
at the surface and on the sandbanks
of blue and orange. Ultra-violet dimly
through limestone, frosted with columnals,

glistening in the fiction of our pebble
incline.

Her come-spangled highlight continuous
through all living creatures in the naked
morning spectra. Nomenclature of rivulets,
the slow organic branchings of the glass
machinery in the ravine incalculable. Coal
solidifies to be eroded later into a curious
stone terminator line. Mute and recoiled
in some hollow interglacial autumn.
Its reflection in the lake a microclimatic
inclusion of our monotonous dream light.
Asphalt oozes out of the cock
into the spreading liquid fire. Storm
at night in our breathing that flowered
all of beneath into a summer glen.
We portray ourselves perfectly, a single
divine skill. Summer copper dusted
pale green from dusk. Hand lightly
over her left breast if you see it. Evening
cicadas. Night elm corridors – the frozen
manifold a green instrument.

August refracted through her nipples
glazed and wrinkled. The light
in these afternoons as distant nighthawks
beckon those who can tell dawn from dusk.
Delight tantric and warm the electric
mirage loomed a dazzling currency,
the water a quick molecular sand.

There is a path for her nipples erect ozone
the form of the graceful uncorrupt
of another. Distant tropical cicadas
translated it perfectly. In the heart of fall
there is a slow motion of haze. Paris
was there before the evening, silver down
underneath. The forest is filled with nostrils,
genitals, hands and formulates
its own disguises. The light in this first
humid cobalt storm wind. Spring trances
in the control emerald night. An intrusion
of love solidifies beneath the Polaroid
receding blue sky. Giant Scarborough bluffs.

Nomenclature of rivulets, the etched
crystal of erosion. The valley filled
with a Sassafras grove sun through clear
warm water. Eyes, ears and mouth the wind
parted. There is a home in the feet. Her face
vigilant in the night elm corridors.
The valley filled with the wind soft thunder
in our ears. Her pelvis vaulted light.
The night in these afternoons slips into pale
bat wings, night corrupt of another. Distant
tropical panel bobbing phosphorescent
in the heat storm. White violet flickering
slow motion wind of haze and golden
the forest staggered omni-directional. Lobed

canopy occasionally west of Paris, London
is two thousand evenings, silver down.

A consensual domain in the summer
wasteland. June, limestone village parks
transform into mouths, glistening lacunae
in an arena. Multi-foliate her orgasms curl
and vanish into the landscape. Tall elms,
sensual detail rippling through coal
and limestone smoke around the year 1908.
Electric gradients motionless in the stadium
heat zone of her touching. Sunset
glistening marble with milk snakes
and milk sliding couples.

There can be no highlights in an ancient
museum where the walls depict no
reflections, no rainbows. The rendition
of a forest dependent. Slickensided fluting
of feet on packed soil, her flesh on humus
shimmering like no other. There is nothing
arbitrary in the predestined universe
of the past. Her squatting all night, slowly
in the night wind, their toadstools
emerging right up into her vagina. Pale
water. Distant red glow budding right up
into her, her molluscan hydrogen pumps.
Crouching in the amphibious June clarity
and support of summer sky. Salamander's
vibrato through the moist forest beneath
rocks. Humus without witness, without

the secret harmony of insects. Space
solidifies into limestone over the path.
Blue fluid support of the sum perpetual
memory of a life-unit. Trapped explorations
of sexual forests. The dim pop
of an exploding weather Zonde clicks
in the high thin air, an intangible barrier.

The clarity of aerospace suspends the lactose
silk of her breasts. Contrail, no clouds,
no earth. An interlocking network of pure
wisdom. Corridors of gigantic elms
glittering in the windows of August. Moss
and rain on limestone obliquely over
the pitcher plants. In the next tent, dimly,
it all happens quite rapidly. Throughout
the land could be heard the sound
of weeping babies, honeycombed
with entrances, preparing to be born
from the points of molluscoid teats.
A theatre of bark, a large room
if there is no point of view. The virtual
image is pure subject, wallpapered
in a stage rendition. The forest is naked.
The pad of feet on the terminator line,
evening stars, nipples erect stuck bits
of leaf to. Velvet theatre curtains
undulating after having a large toadstool
emerge to the north. Orange toadstool
of immense budding right into glacial clay
bluffs and the narrow pool.

The evening unfolds itself in silence
and without witness, naked waists in cool
stone shiver each time the sum perceptual
memory realizes the planet's dream. Image
without recognition in the sediments.
The dim pop of a weather Zonde
surrounding her. The forest is an air
of the ionosphere. Slim curve of her waist.
Leaves of the rhododendron through
the sulphur water clarity. Corridors
of gigantic elms, Egyptian gradients
in the anticipation of August.

Only the brightest stars glowing
in the dry whispering celluloid
hills. Air foetuses billowing like the desert
night, their water-brains open enough
for the detail. Thought impulses
and thunder my fingers water dispersing
porous into the land. The insects gather
at night with their bases just below
the regalia of summer foliage, this meaning
haze and slanting rays of the pit vipers.
The two pilots sweat with grotesque electric
contrails. There is a peace at this point,
a powdery luminescence of grass.
The insects gather at night beneath the trees.
And touching you were that my claims

by dreaming but illusions that lay waste
the foliage of your nervous system. Infra-
red snakes sway in a phantasmic waveform.
Niagara inebriates the eyes, the granular
phrasing of her invertebrate orgasms. Like
some hand or shadow, each sound rings
in the silent free-fall through the words.
Under the swells a heat wave submerges
the river vegetation in the source
of neural conductivity.

The water glistens dully, intrigued
by the sexual options. Cocks and nipples
and the Springbank catalogue. Her eyes
ascribe to electric tendrils through
the Hungry Hollow hills, memory vapour.
Her, nervously. The storybook blue night
converges and hovers just beyond the trees
in Victoria park, sperm barely opaque
in the haze. The semi-transparent foliage
of veins and huge scarab beetles, iridescent
under the camera tree. Night siphons
the cascade of night and night wind coming
nervously drugged and cool. Only
the regalia of summer foliage. A wind stirs
the fissure of camouflage, of expectant
magnification. A distant blue jay sounds
the tension. The precision of an albino fox
in the cedar verge. In sleep they are waves
within breathing at night in the desert,
the air distant momentums. Surges linger

enough for the detail. Her children
the lake claims by dreaming, water
dispersing porous into the armoured spinal
chord. Pulsing thrill formed as a sphere
around it. The ammonites a copper mist
gleaming in a mute bell of psilocybic
thickness.

The earth reaches up thin lissome arms
and legs trailing areolisma. Fierce array
of the golden summer instruction dictated
by deafening cicadas. Her parents
obviously indicated by detail, open
at either end. The planets converge
in the evening sky. Swollen lips in the full
noon sun, cocks, electromagnetic fields.
Translucent heads the cool vagina wing-
covers and fabulous horns. Drugged
cascade of mirror and chrome rising into
itself from the living-room window. Free-
fall reaches us in thin pulsing spinal thrills.

Ripples indicate the fertility of the white
elm, night dragons deep within. Black
River cicada through the brassy July sky.
Spring trances in the propagation lee
of the glass machinery. Preserved in stone
as molecular evening stars ascending over

the observatory. An orange patch of sun
opaque in the vacancy of pubescent night
traffic. Sand flats silent to this kingdom's
maze. Feeding hairline crack a barn-storm
device approaches like a blind-spot.
The forest rejoices in the sound of distant
waves. Hissing intentions. The choice
conceived by her witnessing. In the next
tent, dimly, the workings of the unseen
machinations. Electro-chemicals
are the horizon exposing memory, high
with endless erotic throttles withstanding
erosion. Bats are wafted by chains of small
words. A lax penis spewing sperm
into the night sky. Orange limestone,
Persian Milky Way and forest. Symphonies
in the distant mulberry tunnels and open
pavilions beside the river under budding
thickets of night. The sound strobes
into star clusters, rain-tires on the evening
bridge. All thresholds detail the single
crystal of genetic solar irradiation. Juice
flowing sustained by her apartments
and older women not yet quietly offering
dreams. The sun renewed through
the articulation and splendour
of our prodigious evolution.

Watch your own face decay under
the sounds of weeping you have spawned
in her. The forest's strange progeny

of a rainless storm. Only the blue
megahertz evening in the retina
of a Mayan astronomer. The nighthawks
transmitted through the moist air
like no others.

Softly glowing veins of opalized
limestone and spring sky, the matrix
evaporating. Burning the river dry
the shadow moving through the words.
Interface of limestone fluorescing
in the depths clairvoyant like a kind
of relief. The yellow jackets are alien
wholeness on bending and illumined hot
metals. In August there is a second
choreography. Fossils are brought
into a very neural humour, the physical
residues of previous occurrence. In a dream
glowing arrays of molecules execute slow
gyrations near the surface of the organism.
The pool is vacuous to the predatory night
breezes. One exists both in it and outside
the chrysalis cases. All the observers
are translucent blue, stuffed saran masses
of hieroglyphics. After these alien
and bending days is the silent summer.
Nighthawks, the absence of other humans
and the cold sun of September. Magnolias

moving through the words to such a small
extent that by looking through them
one exists in the undergrowth. Striped
recurring sequence. At night some hand
or choice moves, the pool is perhaps
shimmering, opaque star jelly. How easily
in the next tent, dimly constricted
as if your name had been a kind of passage
of figures, is a relief formed.

Hanging gardens ceaselessly dark
at the bottom where jewels in the hollow
oak's loam form an undecipherable mass.
Deity being the council of dreams
in a display herald for the thousand perfect
intrinsic faces, themselves perspectivized
into a white, convergent evolution.
In Brasilia the rude honest eyes
of the observers fall upon the machinery,
poised and glistening in the forest.
How easily the invisible camera shifts
a contracting pupil of magic around
the sourceless light of surveillance.
A cavern about him composed of foliage
and stones. During the day the pond
increased into green. Sweating bannisters
are the only concrete manifestations
of memory.

The pool is perhaps horizontal over
our heads. Buds emerge red, randomly

illuminating the lower boughs
of the pawpaw triumphant. At twilight
harlequin nocturne. All the invisible
cameras shift into our eyes. Deep
in the light field of the city. Metaphorical
objects, the mood of foliage and stones,
are fictional labyrinths of synesthesia,
mimics of the virtual inhabitants.

Blonde and shimmering, the evening eye
twists under strong winds. Halfway
up the side of bleached elaborate horns
and attachments. And yet the tiny field
within the music is blown glass and cruelty.
It all happens quite rapidly. Local
scarabaeidae elaborate the vast machinery
of the stars. There are sections where each
house encloses a novel dusk.

When I see her flesh budding
I am limestone streams. Fireflies, agile
in their nervous evacuation of dreams.
Memory succubus old as the moon ascends
behind Arkona. She is fair, she is dark
with moonlit fields. Her unearthly children
rise up into your eternal existence in sunlit
replicas of herself. The stars are perhaps
mistakes swarming through the canopy

of the broken consort, their branches
a nocturnal heat storm. The body is a large
yellow ochre terraced command,
a reconstruction of the word. In the city,
which is a composed stratosphere
of moonlight high over Dundas, the street
cars and trains almost run a small
passenger airliner lost in the sidewalks.
Pedestrians must sometimes dangle
in ever rising cascades. There are stones
over the garden wall, one soon loses
the sensation of falling. The anvil
is nearby. There is a long descent
to the river which is a rumour written
in smoke. The boulevard homes glitter
with stained desire. The trestle a slow-
motion avalanche proceeding
to the opposite side beneath the trees
sustained as bats' desire. A hot moist
climate engenders the river, a shock-wave
of mist trees. One of the train tracks does
not descend an infra-red jungle of thermal
ridges but instead runs past the park
and museum in a perfect triangular
fossil-jawed replica.

Genital clusters, leaf groin of digestion.
She is Hungry Hollow, a translucent
Saturn. She supervises wet dreams
in the vacant observatory. The underwater
paradigm of amber and flash white

into night sky brook chambers. Bend sinister
composes its entirety of interlocking gold
rings and amulets. Tactile revelation of stone
bridges and the dream city. Tops
of cumulonimbus graze the hills
of the opposite bank where Mattawa stands.
Rivers of cool air flow through glass
windows depicting vague ravines.
The body is a slow fire, a level plain
out over the contours.

The envelope of consciousness surrounds
a labyrinth of small parks and stone
outcroppings. Small creeks course through
the majesty of earthquakes. The internal
summer a tender flood. Her nipples stiffen
away from ourselves. Her delicate white
metallic night. Bridges, streams
and limestone nucleotides.

The exoskeleton is a desperate dream
in this woodlot. A light impossibly
orange coming on over the shopping plaza.
Even the planets are motile, as slime molds
slide under the smoked glass sunset. Skin
divers nervously explore this tanned skin,
the village streets technologized by moths
fluttering on tissue, flitting shadows.

The period gardens, their scale-speed
thermal conglomerates of cool and warm.
Stone night. Stars arbitrate the carnivorous
solar dictation. Small creeks course
through the sky no longer enclosing
us. Tanned skin aglow and each muscle
is a universe where what we consider
uncanny reflects unnecessarily
on the flashing metal scuttling beneath.
Frequently furniture is vacant of figures,
space constricted by the passage of time.
Vector obsolescent the erectile blue
bandshell night tunnel. Stone spider web.
Field of the moon.

The streets wind fragile in the rarefied air
of bridges, streams, and limestone rock
chapel orange and red. The concrete seal-
pools and ox-bows. Earth. The airplane's
engine blossoming in the ominous roar
of a flash flood. Eels are pulled
from the canal. We are just a step away
from the evening, hoary with diamonds.
Gasoline sunsets burst through smoked
lamps, giant mantids above moist rain-
shower humus. The quiet stars splash out
of the cutaneous telephoto insignia, lush
moon with lavender areola. The expectant
interglacial universe. Bats investigate
houses as they would the carnivorous
writhing of cycads. Cecropia moths flutter

on refractive distortions. Wet foliage
in large fragments at the base of the pool.

Summer dawn at London airport.
The further trees open to gardens on both
levels into dream at visual horizon.
Q.E.W. reflects the radar-dish, still
in the morning's ascension. The red
dawn, orange against Persian blue,
charmed particles of dusk.

Unnatural grace of fast night clouds.
The hot wind unrestrained into her urgent
gold. Her skin palace cool devon cream,
a sparse necklace, and we are just a step
away from ourselves. Thick spurting moth
tunnels traced by pheromones,
their delicate choreography. Abdominal
trails behind the snow clouds. Advance
greens darkly traced in a silence implied
by the shadows of the light grey limestone.
Torroidal nets. Faint shadow on the date
palm delineating the hover fly. Staggered
grace the distant low fountains of synthetic
envelopes. Marble tiled rose-grottos
and burnt amber shimmering with altitude,
with distance. The impossible dolomite
cliffs, foliage boiling into the city.
The woodlots straining like mesas
for visible movement in the wind.
The impossible, iridescent flower beetles

lying in crawling fear of the words being
formed in the early morning light.
A woman crying inside the perfect fossil
of an unknown diode. The lions
and unicorns that later in May
are arraigned through the visual scan
of our fingers. Hidden in vegetation
and haze, their statuary straining in terror,
almost achieving fireflies. Lips are drawn
over the teeth glowing red and green.
Absolute July sun on the white herald
of the anti-dawn. There are sections
where the children leave the larvae alone.

The air warm yet quickened with espionage
and silver. Air thick with allusion.
The puffy silent flight of the coastal
twilight. Cisterns full of dark tannin, words
from silence hatched. Limestone endless
in detail and its surface glistening
with paraboloids. Ethereal blue thick mist
of the escarpment streaming down silently
on all this. Cathedrals and botanical
lithographic stone. Beaded skin over
the first fine figments of ice on endless
Haiku plains.

Night trains and the transparent
cecropia moths aimlessly copulating,
frictionless, just beyond our reflection
in her budding cellular flesh. Limestone
endless in detail under the hot overcast
swamp vision.

Linnaeus delineating our most habitual
routes. Autoclave, the exposed limestone
of the Paris valley becomes the pebble
beach of Tyrconnell. Nighthawks vigilant
through the awesome humus, exotic insects
splashing dank luminous perfumes.
Multifoliate her orgasms beneath
the orange glow of farmhouse windows,
aquariums damp with emergence.

Electric neo-carboniferous glow. Oil and gas
flow from the zone of her touching.
Looking beyond to the lactose silk
of her breasts in the summer night.
Panavistic crystal blades slice through
boulders. Fossils are silhouetted
for an instant. Image without recognition
to lay on the tracks. I must be crushed
by surrounding her. Fossils are dragged
from the points of molluscoid teats,
streaming like the unrelenting hunger
of her night. Old mahogany furniture
rotting into glacial clay bluffs and a narrow
garden terrace. At noon the exposed

limestone is a mathematical plain
in critical grey light, a parabolic reflector
of atmospheric space for Cenozoic
bivalves. Runaway metamorphosis
of insects proceeds. Leaves realizing
the planet's dream.

The sweet desert of soul spreading
into the city. Our seasons do not
contaminate the beaches. The summer sun
low and softly stabbing the weird music
of the stars. The continuum in summer
is a mature distant amphetamine
lovemaking. A white subtropical forest. End
of the sparkling glass northern mineshaft
star cathedral. I am a certain woman, in this
she approaches the coastal twilight. Barely
pubescent my breasts are cool at the surface
and warm beneath. Pink, some feline
vagina. The lynx padded dimly through
the tree ferns. Perfect mid-air suspended
vortex of wing and flesh burning pink
and blue and orange cool granular cork
over her budding cellular lightning.

The glass machinery intact as if it itself
were against the screen door. Sunny
harpsichord forest morning dimly around

the curve of this afternoon. As if paradise
renewed each other's symmetry. Yes,
we are an electronic grey day over lake
Huron. Glistening dark beautiful wings
against the summers that were. Words
from silence hatched. She approaches
me shyly at the edge of the apartment
building. We have always made love
like the constellations. Empty sunlit
building rotting into the September soil.
A stonehouse chiaroscuro of yellow
holding forth its Polaroid blue and white
Lawren Harris. Mysterious nocturnal
waves of lake Erie on white sand, foam
phosphorescing in the moonlight.
Montreal submerged just beyond
inexplicable childhood memories.
There is no season, there are no ledges
and the wall descends a storm at night
in our breathing. Serotonin drips
from the calculations.